AF574774

Go and Get It!

Jane Langford
Illustrated by Teri Gower

Spike had a stick.
He wanted to play with it.

"Go and get the stick!" said Dad.

Spike had a ball.
He wanted to play with it.

"Go and get the ball!" said Dad.

Spike had a bone.
He wanted to play with it.

"Go and get the bone!"
said Dad.

Spike saw a cat.
He wanted to play with it.

"Go and get the dog!" said Mum.